DUE 11/23

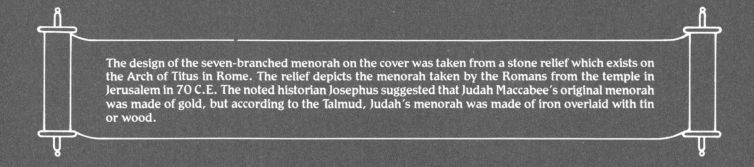

The design of the seven-branched menorah on the cover was taken from a stone relief which exists on the Arch of Titus in Rome. The relief depicts the menorah taken by the Romans from the temple in Jerusalem in 70 C.E. The noted historian Josephus suggested that Judah Maccabee's original menorah was made of gold, but according to the Talmud, Judah's menorah was made of iron overlaid with tin or wood.

אוצרות חנוכה

TREASURES
OF
CHANUKAH

INTRODUCTION

To see the happy gleam in children's eyes, reflecting the glow of Chanukah candles kindled at home as the whole joyous family joins in song, is to behold a miracle. This miracle is born of the miracle related in the Talmud (the vast post-Biblical treasure of Jewish law and lore completed in the seventh century of our era).

The Talmud tells us that when the Syrian-Greek King Antiochus Epiphanes installed a pagan altar to Zeus in the Holy Temple in Jerusalem, a rebellion broke out. A handful of Maccabeans gathered many followers and challenged the powerful Syrian-Greek army. They won battle after battle with bare hands and stones against the armored troops. Finally they won in Jerusalem. The happy heroes raced into the Temple, dashed Zeus to pieces, and sought the sacred oil to light up the Temple and to re-consecrate it (that's the English meaning of Chanukah) to the worship of the One God of mankind. They found but one little cruse of unpolluted oil sufficient but for a single day. Now came the miracle. The consecrated oil lasted for eight days.

So for over 2,000 years now the Jewish people have been celebrating the Maccabean victory and kindling Chanukah candles for eight nights, one on the first, two on the second and on progressively to eight on the final evening of Chanukah.

The miracle, of course, rises from the historical facts; the events in the Holy Land from 168-165 B.C.E. It really marks the miracle of the victory of the few over the many, the weak over the strong, those of pure faith over those of pagan faith.

Winning the victory of freedom of religion provided the human family with a key to the ultimate victory of political freedom — human rights over all the One World governed by the One Creator — a victory yet to be won.

The happy gleam in children's eyes as they kindle the Chanukah candles is not only something of a miracle to behold and to remember. It is also a reflection of a hope and an inspiration.

This beautiful treasure-trove of a book lights up all our eyes with the joy of Chanukah.

Rabbi Ely E. Pilchik

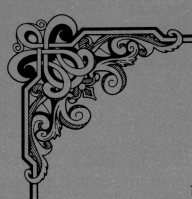

PUBLISHER'S ACKNOWLEDGEMENTS

I would like to take this opportunity on behalf of myself, Greg Hildebrandt, and the entire Unicorn Publishing staff to thank the following people for their time, effort, knowledge, and continued encouragement during the research and making of this book. Without their help, achieving the historical and religious accuracy of Treasures of Chanukah would have been an overwhelming task.

Jean L. Scrocco
Publisher

Paul H. Blumenthal

Mary Slater

Bernice Slater

Melvin Slater

Rabbi Ely E. Pilchik
Rabbi Emeritus, Temple B'nai Jeshurun, Short Hills, NJ

Rabbi Joshua Goldstein
Spiritual Leader of Temple Sha'arey Shalom, Springfield, NJ

Rabbi Israel Gordon
of the Rabbinical College of America, Morristown, NJ

ACKNOWLEDGEMENTS

My deepest thanks to all my friends who posed for the characters in
this edition of *Treasures of Chanukah*, enabling me to recreate the origin
and joys of this festive holiday.

CAST OF CHARACTERS

Paul H. Blumenthal — Mattathias
Michael A. Backer, Esq. — Judah Maccabee
Daniel Slater — Mattathias' Son
Jeff Weinstein — Mattathias' Son, Hasidic Rabbi
Robert L. Rebach — Mattathias' Son, Citizen of Modin, Maccabean Soldier
Larry Weiss — Mattathias' Son, Citizen of Modin, Maccabean Soldier
Jim Osmond — Statue of Zeus
Doris Vallejo — Citizen of Jerusalem
Andrea Zugale — Citizen of Jerusalem
Joseph Kubert — Citizen of Jerusalem, Maccabean Soldier
Matthew Zugale — Citizen of Jerusalem, Child with Dreydl
Larry Spiegel — Citizen of Modin
Jim Settel — Citizen of Modin
Boris Vallejo — Greco-Syrian Soldier
Greg Hildebrandt — Greco-Syrian Soldier
Greg Hildebrandt Jr. — Greco-Syrian Soldier
Carl Drozdowicz — Greco-Syrian Soldier
Joseph D. Scrocco Jr. — Greco-Syrian Soldier
Todd Jaeger — Greco-Syrian Soldier
Bill Golliher — Greco-Syrian Soldier
Jackie Slater — Mother
Stephen Solomon — Father
Mary Slater — Grandmother
George Ginsberg — Grandfather
Jaime Michele Bedrin — Daughter
Garret Scott Bedrin — Son
Samantha Weinstein — Baby Daughter
Melvin Slater — Priest with Shofar, High Priest, Citizen of Jerusalem
Bernice Slater — Mother by piano
Gerri Weinstein — Daughter playing piano
Jodi Green — Daughter by piano
Martin Green — Rabbi
Daniel Zugale — Haesedic Child, Child with Dreydl

LIST OF ILLUSTRATIONS

The Idol of King Antiochus
Mattathias Pulls Down the Heathen Altar
Mattathias is Gathered to His Fathers
Judah Maccabee Battles Like a Lion
The Dedication of the Altar
The Miracle of the Holy Lamps
The Lighting of the First Candle
The Special Treats of Chanukah
The Joy of Giving
The Magic of the Dreydl
The Tale of the Maccabees is Told
The Tiny Flickering Lights
Rock of Ages
Kindle the Taper
Mattathias
My Dreydl
Mi Yemalel
Y'mey HaHanukah
Candle Lights
Blessings Over the Lights

The design of the seven-branched menorah on the cover was taken from a stone relief which exists on the Arch of Titus in Rome. The relief depicts the menorah taken by the Romans from the temple in Jerusalem in 70 C.E. The noted historian Josephus suggested that Judah Maccabee's original menorah was made of gold, but according to the Talmud, Judah's menorah was made of iron overlaid with tin or wood.

This book is dedicated to peace.

אוצרות חנוכה

TREASURES OF CHANUKAH

The Unicorn Publishing House
New Jersey

Designed and Edited by Jean L. Scrocco
Associate Juvenile Editor: Heidi K.L. Corso
Music consultant: Dale Trimmer
Printed in Singapore by Singapore National Printers Ltd through Palace Press
Typography by L&B Typo of NYC, New York, NY
Reproduction photography by The Color Wheel, New York, NY

◆ ◆ ◆ ◆ ◆

◆ ◆ ◆ ◆ ◆

Distributed in Canada by Doubleday Canada Ltd., Toronto, ON M5B 1Y3, Canada
Distributed in the rest of the world by World Wide Media Service, Inc., New York, NY

◆ ◆ ◆ ◆ ◆

Special thanks to Yoh Jinno, Joe Scrocco, Bill McGuire, Kathy Pizar, Bob Rebach and
the entire Unicorn staff.

◆ ◆ ◆ ◆ ◆

Printing History 15 14 13 12 11 10 9 8 7 6 5 4 3 2

◆ ◆ ◆ ◆ ◆

Library of Congress Cataloging in Publication Data
Treasures of Chanukah.
Summary: Presents a collection of songs, stories, poems, and prayers in celebration of Hanukkah.
1. Hanukkah — Juvenile literature. [1. Hanukkah]
l. Hildebrandt, Greg, ill.
BM695. H3T74 1987 296.4'35 87-10802
ISBN 0-88101-071-5

The Story of the Maccabees

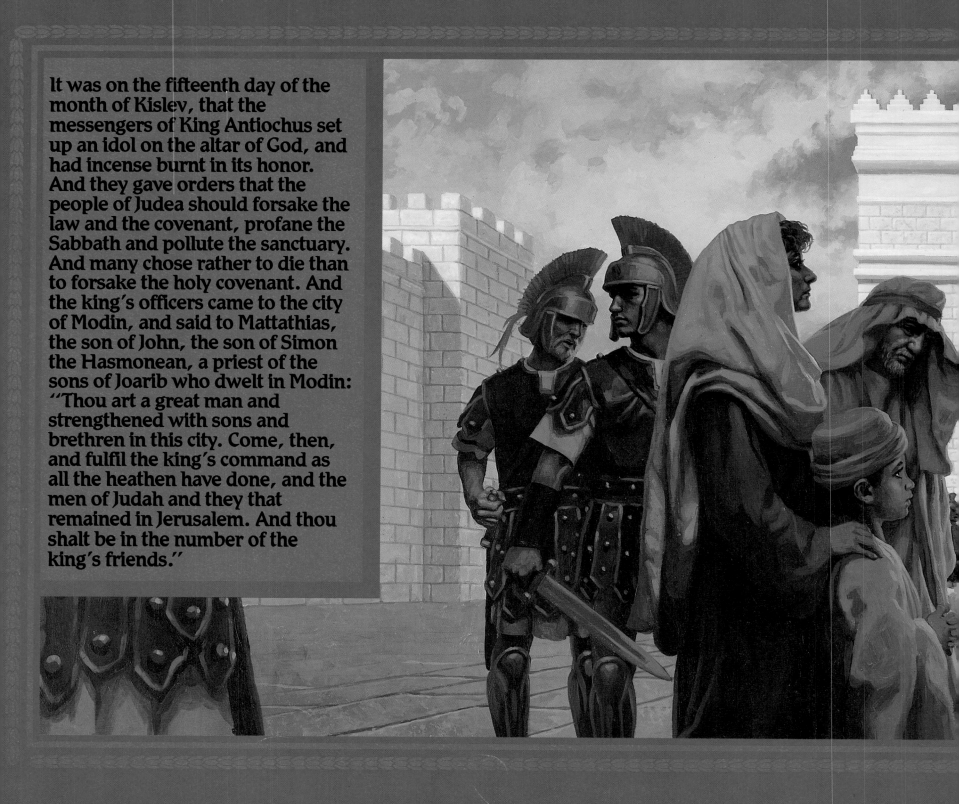

It was on the fifteenth day of the month of Kislev, that the messengers of King Antiochus set up an idol on the altar of God, and had incense burnt in its honor. And they gave orders that the people of Judea should forsake the law and the covenant, profane the Sabbath and pollute the sanctuary. And many chose rather to die than to forsake the holy covenant. And the king's officers came to the city of Modin, and said to Mattathias, the son of John, the son of Simon the Hasmonean, a priest of the sons of Joarib who dwelt in Modin: "Thou art a great man and strengthened with sons and brethren in this city. Come, then, and fulfil the king's command as all the heathen have done, and the men of Judah and they that remained in Jerusalem. And thou shalt be in the number of the king's friends."

But Mattathias answered and spake with a loud voice: "Though all the nations that are under the king's dominion obey him and fall away each one from the religion of his fathers, yet will l and my sons and my brethren walk in the covenant of our fathers. God forbid that we should forsake the law to depart from our faith either to the right hand or the left." And when in the sight of all one of the Jews came to sacrifice to the idol, Mattathias was inflamed with zeal, neither could he forbear to show his anger, and he slew him, and also the king's officer, and the altar he pulled down. And Mattathias cried throughout the city with a loud voice saying: "Whosoever is zealous of the law and maintaineth the covenant, let him follow me." So he and his sons fled into the mountains, and they went about pulling down the heathen altars, and they rescued the law out of the hands of the Gentiles.

And the days of Mattathias drew near that he should die and he said to his sons: "Be ye zealous for the law and give your lives for the covenant of your fathers. Remember what our fathers did in their generations. Was not Abraham found faithful in temptation, and it was accounted to him for righteousness? Phineas, our father, for that he was zealous exceedingly, obtained the covenant of an everlasting priesthood. David, for being faithful, inherited the throne of a kingdom forever and ever. Throughout all the ages none that put their trust in God were overcome. Therefore be strong, my sons, and show yourselves men in behalf of the law; for therein shall ye obtain glory." And he blessed them and was gathered to his fathers.

Then Judah, called Maccabee, rose up in his stead, and all his brethren aided him, and they fought with gladness the battle of Israel. He battled like a lion and the lawless shrunk for fear of him. He cheered Jacob by his mighty acts, and his memorial is blessed forever. And when all the people feared and trembled at the sight of the great number of the enemy, and said: "What? Shall we be able, being a small company, to fight against so great and so strong a multitude?" Judah answered: "With the God of heaven it is all one to save by many or by few. And all the people shall know that there is One who redeemeth and saveth Israel." And Judah led them into battle, and behold the hosts of the enemy were discomfited before them. And Israel had a great deliverance. And they sang songs of thanksgiving, and praised the Lord of heaven for His goodness, because His mercy endureth forever.

And on the five and twentieth day of Kislev, the same day when three years before the altar of God had been profaned by the heathen, the sanctuary of God was dedicated anew with songs and music, and the people praised the God of heaven who had given them great victory, and they celebrated the Dedication of the Altar for eight days, and there was great rejoicing among the people. Moreover, Judah and his brethren with the whole congregation of Israel ordained that the days of the Dedication of the Altar should be celebrated, from year to year, for eight days in gladness and thanksgiving.

The Festival of Lights

By
Bernice Slater

The festival of lights you know,
is said to be a miracle.
It happened many years ago,
in the land of Israel's people.

Brave Judah led the battle cry,
to deliver up his people,
and raised once more God's altar
with gladness, song, and music.

And they kindled new the holy lamps
and brought to God their offering;
with oil enough for just one night,
for eight days it stood lasting.

And our children still rejoice and dream
of wondrous eves of thanksgiving.
For on each night of Chanukah
a candle shall be lit,
and the family joins together,
each one to celebrate.

And Mother, she prepares and bakes
the latkes and the special cakes,
while Father stacks the presents high,
as wide-eyed children wait nearby.

For on each night of Chanukah
a gift they will receive,
as they praise God's miracle of oil;
in this each one believes.

And the children play a timeless game,
sent down from all the ages.
As the dreydl spins and spins and spins,
the magic is created.
Each child's hope of winning
echoes laughter, joy, and song.
As it softly falls upon the earth,
it seems to take so long.
And the children run up close to see—
oh my, who shall the winner be?

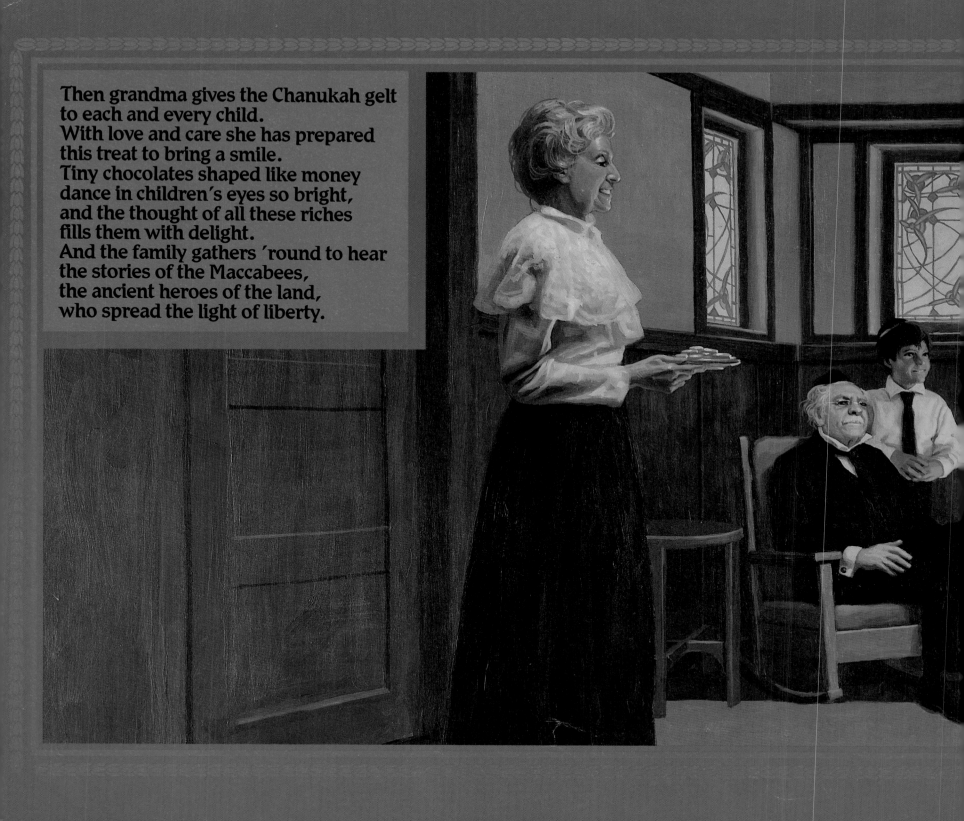

Then grandma gives the Chanukah gelt
to each and every child.
With love and care she has prepared
this treat to bring a smile.
Tiny chocolates shaped like money
dance in children's eyes so bright,
and the thought of all these riches
fills them with delight.
And the family gathers 'round to hear
the stories of the Maccabees,
the ancient heroes of the land,
who spread the light of liberty.

Our menorah is the symbol
of our faith and history,
and through its tiny flickering lights,
our troubles you can see:
the weak that fought the forces
of the powerful tyranny;
the triumph of right over might—
our final victory.

Songs and Blessings

MAOZ TZUR

Gustav Gottheil & M. Jastrow

KINDLE THE TAPER

Emma Lazarus & Jacob Singer

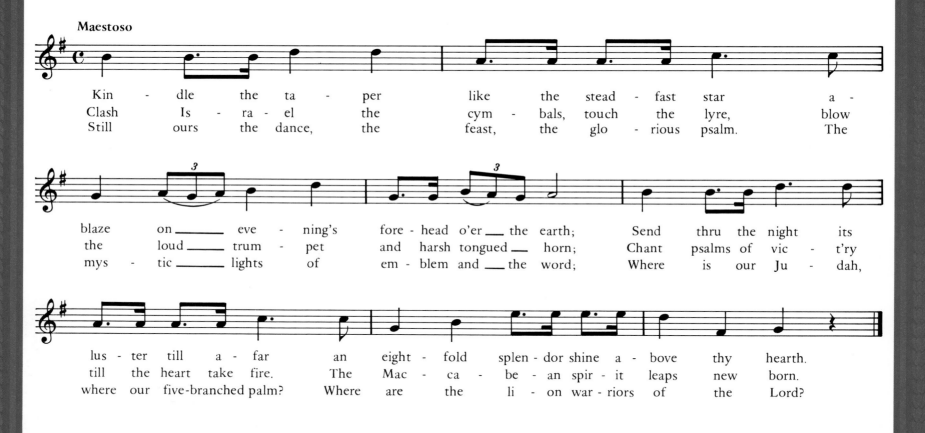

MATTATHIAS

E.E. Levinger & H. Coopersmith

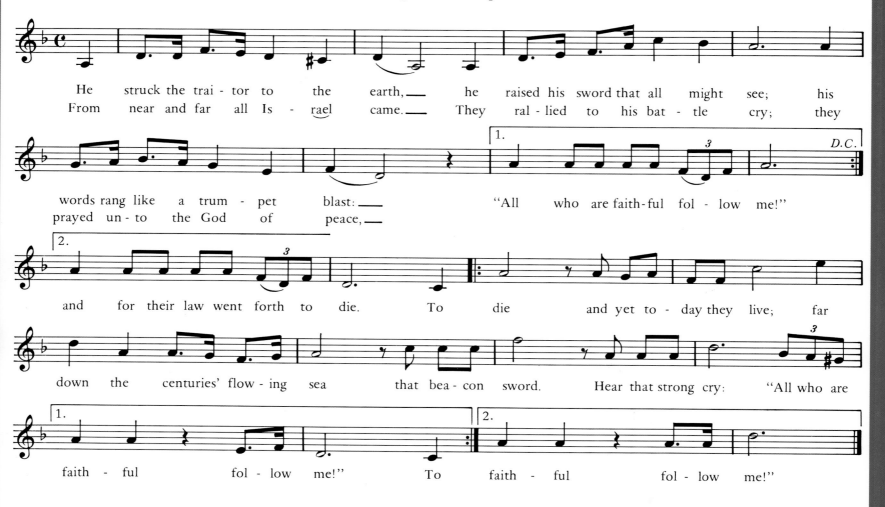

MY DREYDL

Samuel S. Grossman & Samuel E. Goldfarb

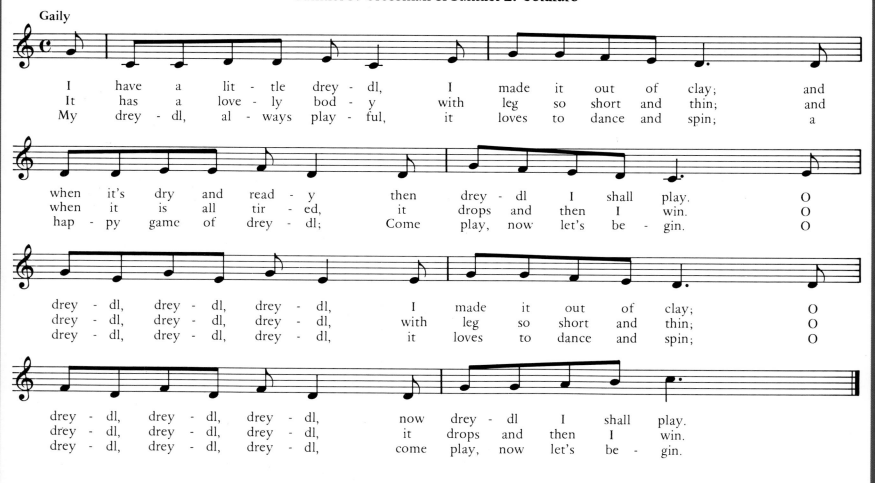

MI YEMALEL

Ben M. Edidin

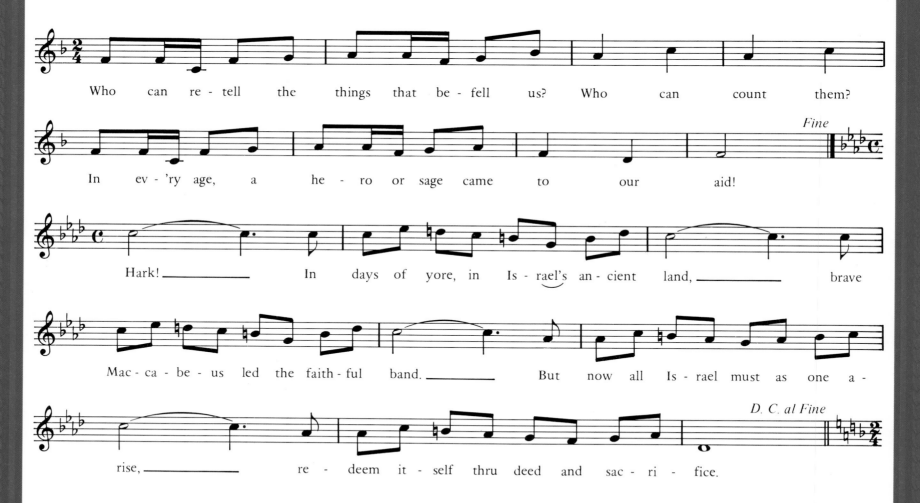

Y'MEY HAHANUKAH

A. Evronin & E. Guthmann

CANDLE LIGHTS

Abraham M. Klein

Dead heroes ride the chariots of the wind;
Jew phantoms light the candles of the sky.
Old war cries echo in my memory;
The ghosts of five brave brothers stalk my mind.
And this because my father and his kind
Are lighting heirloom'd candelabra, aye,
Are singing praises to the One on high,
This night in which past battles are enshrined!
As sweet as were the sweet songs of degrees
That David sang rejoicing, is this rite
My sire rejoicing sings; and as the sight
Of almond blooms that burst on springtime trees
In sight of this menorah, and of these
Eight blossoms breaking on a winter night!

BLESSINGS OVER THE LIGHTS

Praised be Thou, O Lord our God,
Ruler of the world, who hast sanctified us
by Thy commandments, and bidden us
kindle the Hanukkah lights.

Ba·ruch a·ta, A·do·nai E·lo·hei·nu,
me·lech ha·o·lam, a·sher ki·de·sha·nu
be·mits·vo·tav, ve·tsi·va·nu
le·had·lik neir shel Cha·nu·ka.

Praised be Thou, O Lord our God,
Ruler of the world, who didst wondrous things
for our fathers, in days of old,
at this season.

Ba·ruch a·ta, A·do·nai E·lo·hei·nu,
me·lech ha·o·lam, she·a·sa ni·sim
la·a·vo·tei·nu ba·ya·mim ha·heim
ba·ze·man ha·zeh.

Praised be Thou, O Lord our God,
Ruler of the world, who hast granted us life,
sustained us, and permitted us to celebrate
this joyous festival.

Ba·ruch a·ta, A·do·nai E·lo·hei·nu,
me·lech ha·o·lam, she·he·che·ya·nu
ve·ki·ye·ma·nu ve·hi·gi·a·nu
la·ze·man ha·zeh.

In the traditional blessings over the Chanukah lights, all three
verses are recited on the first night. The first two verses are
spoken on each of the following seven nights.

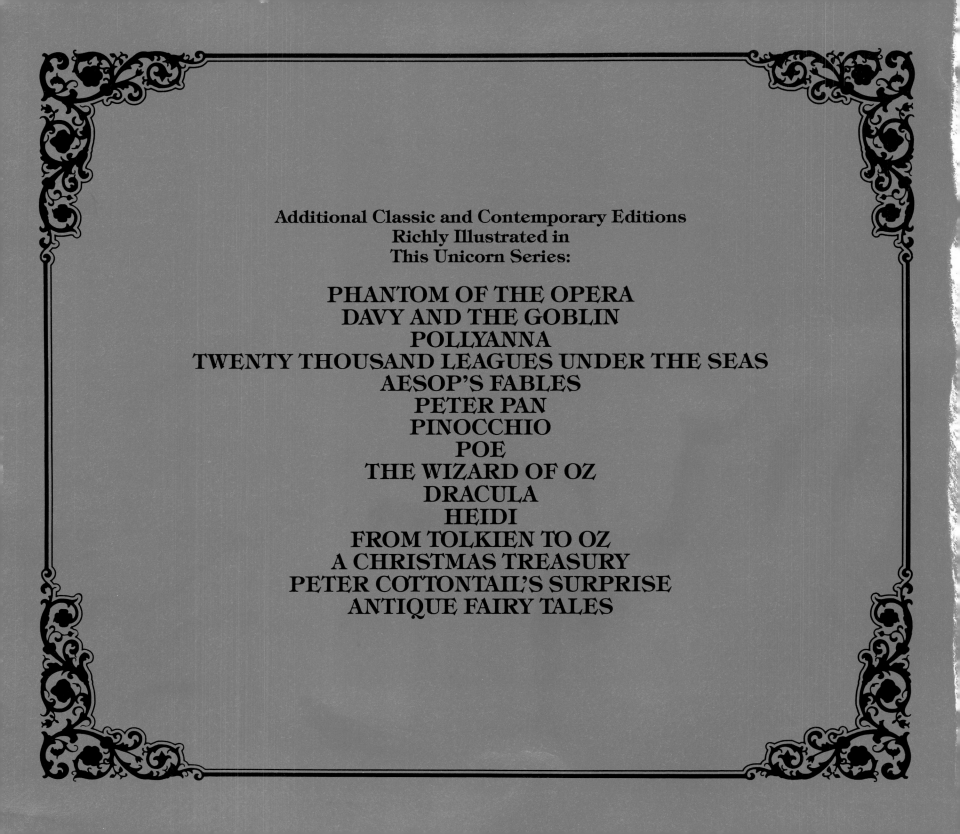

Additional Classic and Contemporary Editions
Richly Illustrated in
This Unicorn Series:

PHANTOM OF THE OPERA
DAVY AND THE GOBLIN
POLLYANNA
TWENTY THOUSAND LEAGUES UNDER THE SEAS
AESOP'S FABLES
PETER PAN
PINOCCHIO
POE
THE WIZARD OF OZ
DRACULA
HEIDI
FROM TOLKIEN TO OZ
A CHRISTMAS TREASURY
PETER COTTONTAIL'S SURPRISE
ANTIQUE FAIRY TALES